Pinda was the Richest Little Girl

Linda Silva Evans

Archway Publishing books may be ordered through booksellers or by contacting:

Archway Publishing
1663 Liberty Drive
Bloomington, IN 47403
www.archwaypublishing.com
844-669-3957

Interior Image Credit: Linda Silva Evans

ISBN: 978-1-6657-4334-1 (sc)
      978-1-6657-4336-5 (hc)
      978-1-6657-4335-8 (e)

Library of Congress Control Number: 2023908077

Print information available on the last page.

Archway Publishing rev. date: 05/04/2023

Pinda was the Richest Little Girl

As a young girl, Pinda spent much time with her family. There were trips to the lake weekly.

Where she would swim and play the whole day through.

They would stay until evening time and have dinner there as well.

Her Mom would pack up a yummy salad, rice
pilaf and shishkebobs on the grill. Pinda
felt so rich with all the love; she collected
on those days, a Ruby!

There were trips to the shore, about every weekend.

Where she would body surf in the ocean, bask in the golden sun, and collect shells.

Play games on the boardwalk, eat yummy
food like pizza, corn on the cob and mussels.

Pinda felt so rich with all the sunshine and
love, she collected on those days, Gold
and a Ruby!

There were trips to the Delaware Water Gap.

Where they would take canoe trips down
the river, and fish and camp. The water so
clear, an emerald green, you could see the
fish swim by. Camp at night was warm by
the glow of a topaz fire.

Pinda felt so rich with all the beauty of nature and all the love, she collected on those days, an

Emerald, Topaz and a Ruby!

There were trips to the country farms,
where they would buy bags full of juicy
red apples, tomatoes and golden corn.

The long rides in the country were filled with sights of blue skies, green fields and pastures. Song, daydreams and wonder.

Pinda felt so rich with all the love and adventure, she collected on those days, Gold, Emeralds, · Sapphires and a Ruby!

There were trips to go skiing. A drive to get there made it a days adventure.

They would arrive and have peanut butter and marshmallow fluff sandwiches before their start. Skiing down the trails, the views were so beautiful. Tall, wide, Jade green, evergreens. The snow glistening in the golden sun, reflected little sparkles, like diamonds.

The joy and challenge of racing freely down the hillside was such an excitement.

Pinda felt so rich with all the outdoor beauty, fun and all the love. She was especially happy those times, because she collected on those days, the most precious, Diamonds, Emeralds, Jade, Gold and a Ruby!

Pinda always felt so rich from all her precious memories with her family, like precious gems...her gems...her memories of all the love her family shared!

Pinda felt like she was the richest girl in the whole world...and she was!